Forward:

Sit down a wee while and worry not.

Nothing in nature is perfect, but everything is beautiful.

Remember this as you read this book.
That all nature is working hard for us and the planet

Ellen O'Brien
Author

All rights reserved; no part of this publication may be reproduced
or transmitted by any means, electronic, mechanical, photocopying or
otherwise, without the prior permission of the publisher.
First Published in Great Britain in 2023
Goliath Publishing
This edition first published in 2023

Copyright © 2023 Goliath Publishing
Cover photo and all pictures enclosed Copyright © 2023 Goliath Publishing &
Ellen O'Brien

www.goliathpublishing.co.uk
or
www.goliathpublishing.com

INTRODUCTION

If you are feeling down or you see someone else that is then please talk and if you think you have no-one then ring the Samaritans for free and speak to a person that is trained to listen…

THE SAMARITANS: Call 116 123 for free

If you are a child and need someone to talk to especially if you feel unsafe or depressed then please ring:

Child Line : Call 0800 1111

*Important. The contents of this book are not endorsed by the Samaritans or child Line. However, they are provided in the genuine hope they will be helpful to others.

Dedicated to all on the path of life's great adventure …

ALL the profit from this book is donated to helping these charities.

CONTENTS

Introduction
A Spooky, Wooky, Dookey Day
The Old Granddad Hedgehog
My Three Lovely Amigos
A Letter from Santa
Life on Earth - Pine Cones
Sacred Wheel of Life
A Letter from Santa to Children
The Night Sky : planets, stars and colours
A View From the Top
Great Day out and About
The old Shed/Summerhouse
The First Flower
The Garden
The most beautiful Fairy Soul Essence
Beautiful Day
"Circles Around the Moon"
The Rolling River
The Whistling Wind
Plant
What comes off a flower
Respect
What trees can do
Love
The Earth has a Heartbeat
The sun
A field of snowmen
Peace
Holidays
The Beautiful Horse, Cart and your Future
The Earth's Crust

A SPOOKY, WOOKY, DOOKEY DAY

Oh! It's Friday the 13th September 2019.

It's such a beautiful day and not a cloud in the sky, which is as blue as blue can be. The sun is shining and the birds are singing, so I'm off for a walk, and maybe I'll find some blackberries to pick. I already have cooking apples, and when I come back home later, I'll cook them and make some custard. Then it will be yum, yum to my tum, tum.

As I picked the blackberries in the fields, I ate some of course. They were warm from the sun, and were lovely and sweet. I had to blow a couple of cobwebs off them and give them a brush off with the sleeve of my jumper before putting them in my mouth. There were some red ones too; they were nice and sweet, but not quite ripe.

There were lots of butterflies of different colours all around me and I felt so happy.

Suddenly, a pheasant flew over the hedge and landed by my side. I said, "hello," and we looked at each other for a minute or two before he turned his head and walked along the field picking at the grass as he went. He looked back at me then flew over the hedge to the next field.

I walked on, and was passing a tractor full of hay when I spied a field mouse running about. Oh! I could stay here all day watching the birds, butterflies and bees flying about. The air felt so still, and while I sat there, three young stoats passed in front of me, one behind the other spaced evenly apart. All three turned to look at me, and I laughed and said, "hello" to them. They promptly ran on and went through another hedge. I have never seen anything like it before. Some field mice were scampering about and it was lovely watching them. Now a hare came by, jumping around in the grass. By now I have eaten so many blackberries, that I need to pick some more, so I moved into the next field. A lovely surprise, the gate is open and I don't have to jump over. The farmer must have gone for dinner.

Walking along the field, there was a beautiful tree, with the sun shining through the leaves. There were lots of nuts in the field that had fallen from the tree, and I saw a squirrel foraging about looking for the best nuts. I watched as she packed as many nuts as she could carry into her mouth. She ran to climb the tree, when I saw a movement and noticed three little heads peeking out from a hole in the tree trunk. Unsteadily they climbed out of the nest, which is called a drey, and onto a branch to greet their mother. They were so young, so small, and they clung to the mossy branch with their tiny feet. One baby squirrel lost its balance and fell a little way, but Mam quickly took its head in her mouth and pulled her baby back to safety on the branch to join the others. Then they all went into the tiny nest to eat the nuts. I stayed for a while, wondering if they would come out again, and they did. As I watched, the three little ones played on the tree branch with their mother watching over them, making sure they did not go too far. They knew I was there, and now and then stopped to look at me looking at them. I thought, 'I must get a picture of this', so I took my mobile phone and snapped away while they had fun jumping over each other on the tree branch. The mother taught them as she watched over them just like our mothers do for us.

It was time to walk on and find some more blackberries because I had eaten all I had picked whilst watching the squirrels playing. The blackberries were ripe, and looked lovely in the hedgerows; some were quite big and looked so juicy.

What do we have here? There was another gate, and on the other side were two very fat, Pot Bellied Pigs, lying fast asleep and snoring their heads off. Different coloured chickens were walking about among the pigs, scratching about for food, some drinking from the nearby pig's trough. The pigs were snoring away, deeply asleep, oblivious. I saw the biggest blackberries were at the top of the hedgerow, but I would have to climb onto the gate to try and reach them. I managed to get a few; then, "Oh!" I missed my footing on the gate, and down I fell into the soft, squidgy, stinking, pig slime mixed with cow pat and chicken droppings. Oh my, I didn't feel good!

Who said Friday 13th was unlucky? I have had the best day ever!
When I got home I had a wash and changed my clothes. I cooked my apples and the blackberries I had left; there weren't that many because I had eaten so many of them they were so sweet.

THE OLD GRANDDAD HEDGEHOG

I always keep some of my food back for my hedgehog family, also for the badger (by the way my badger farts a lot!) who comes to see me sometimes when he feels like it. If there is no food for him outside, he bangs his head on the front door. I know it's him, so I go and give him something to eat. He stands back a few feet, and he won't eat it until I go back inside. He will eat most things, but he really loves mashed potato; he likes to drink rainwater. Sadly, I have not been quick enough to take a photograph of him.

The hedgehog family consists of granddad, mam, dad and baby. Granddad has been coming to see me for years; he loves all the food I put out, but his favourite is cheese, chopped up small. He will also eat mashed potato and enjoys Marie and Nice biscuits. Now and again I give him rice. He likes a few drops of milk and will drink rainwater from a bowl. The other night I gave him some cheese, and afterward, he rolled over on one side and started snoring. He was 'out for the count'. After a few minutes he rallied round and ate some more, then he went off up the path. It's lovely to see the family playing together in and out of the flower pots.

So, I wonder if tonight they will eat some blackberries or some apples; they can be very fussy sometimes. They don't like some of the things I buy, but they love coconut!

Most evenings I put food out between ten and eleven-o-clock, which is when the hedgehog family usually come around. At that time it is quiet and people are indoors or in bed. Sometimes, if it is quiet, they might visit around nine-o-clock.

One Friday night, which was on the 13th, I opened the door to put some food out when I couldn't believe what I was seeing; there was a beautiful red and white fox sitting on the step in front of me in the moonlight. There was a clear sky that night, and there was a big, big full moon. The fox did not move as I stepped out to put the food on the grass. I looked behind me to see the lovely moon. Everything was so still, and I could see a few lights shining from the windows of people's homes.

They do not know about what is going on out here, I thought. The fox was still looking at me. I stood very still, and the fox and I stared at each other for about ten minutes; he looked so peaceful and lovely in the moonlight. It was the first time I had seen a fox close up.

After a while, he got up, stretched his hind legs and looked at me before moving away. Strangely, he was not interested in the food. It was such a wonderful feeling that I stayed outside a little while longer. Then, along came all the hedgehog family, and I thought,

'Oh, this has been the best day ever'!

A spooky, dooky, wookey day!

MY THREE LOVELY AMIGOS

I had put some milk out for the cat I call Minnie the Midget by my doorstep, and as I turned to come back into the house, I saw three slugs drinking it.

I came back inside the house after watching all the wonderful wild life in the moonlight. I had talked to all of them, and do you know, they stood or sat listening to me.

They heard me talking to them, but whether they knew what I was saying I don't know. I think they did, so, always say 'hello' to the badger, fox, squirrel, hedgehog, rabbit or the birds; they all can hear you, just like your pet dog or cat.

A LETTER FROM SANTA

Hello Boys and girls all over the world.

This year is a bit different but it will be 'ok'.

All you have to do is write your letter to me and leave it on your table. This year, I have some new reindeer to help, their names are Masie, Ellie and Brooks. They will pick up all your letters and bring them to Santa.

I have been recycling, including myself and my reindeer. Oh! I needed to after all the years going from house to house, village to village, town to town, city to city and county to county all over the world. Ho! ho! ho!, I feel great. Santa's magical Christmas spirit is much quicker and slimmer. (Ahem! I don't think so!) I have Christmas in my step and the reindeer's are looking perky with a spring in their tails and feet ready to whizz off, and take flight. We don't need a chimney to go down now that we are so light, we can go through a closed door, any door, anywhere, so we are coming to see you. Oh, but I shall still need something to eat and drink because I get very hungry and thirsty, so don't forget to leave something, and perhaps some carrots for my reindeer (Santa loves a bun!).

I am coming to see you, so keep looking for me, and listen for my reindeer's bells. Some of you will see me, and I will see you all. Stay safe everyone, and a big, big "thank you" to the NHS and doctors and nurses all over the world.

A Merry Christmas to you all.

Santa

LIFE ON EARTH - PINE CONES

Friday, 13th November 2020.

It was a lovely day as I looked out of the window on walking, I just knew I had to go out to-day and it was to be Porthpean Woods and beach.

I like to put pine cones round my flower pots and plants in the winter; they look good, and the smell is beautiful, earthy and different. Each cone has its own unique smell. There are some fine old fir trees in the woods where there is a good chance cones will have fallen onto the path.

When I arrived at the woods, I noticed a seat and a picnic table so I sat down for a while. No one was around, and it was quiet and peaceful, just lovely; I could hear the waves of the sea nearby. Suddenly, my mobile 'phone rang, and it made me jump. It was my sister in Ireland. A helicopter flew overhead, and I thought it was time to take a walk to my left across the cliffs. From the cliffs, I could see the village and the sea, a truly wonderful view. They was not leading to where the trees were, so I turned back and sat on the seat again. The sun was warm on my face, and the early morning dew was still on the grass.

I was 'told' to look to my right, and I saw many colours reflected in the dew on a circle of grass. Then I was 'told' to put my hands in it, and put it all over my face, which I did, still looking at the beautiful colours glistening in the sunlight. I did this a few times. It felt oh so different, that I didn't want to walk away.

For a while, I sat on the seat, then, as I looked up, as if coming from the sea, there was what looked like a huge crystal, although I knew it wasn't, and I could see the image of a person in the middle. I felt a warm sensation all over, as if I knew who it was - but I didn't. The colours within the crystal were the same as the colours reflected in the dew on the grass, the only difference being that the colours in the crystal were moving, forming different shapes and sizes as it came toward me where I sat. I heard that the earth is within all of us; find what is in the earth and you find yourself. You don't have to travel anywhere, it is all within you. The crystal was as clear and as pure as can be, while all the time moving with colour.

This is nature at its best; a magical, mystical, powerful, truthful, thing to happen.

This left me feeling young and that I could do anything!

Within a few minutes I heard someone talking, and as I turned around I saw two women walking down toward the beach. As they came near I said, "lovely day isn't it?"

After this, I went to the woods and collected some pine cones from under the trees, then, with a spring in my step, I walked toward the beach. There were some steps leading down to the beach, but I did not feel like going all the way down, however, I did take a lovely photograph from the top of the steps. I spoke with some friendly people who were on their way down.

Cool, I thought, this was the best day ever, and I only came out to get some pine cones. One never knows what is in store; nature at its best. I love it.

When I arrived back home, I put the pine cones around my flower pots, and as I did so, I felt as if someone was helping me and I heard them say 'hello'. We need to say 'hello' more often, and pass it on, because if we stop talking and helping each other, we can kiss goodbye to a happy future. Look up at the night sky and see the twinkling, sparkling stars and think how we should all be doing the right thing.

When we do the right thing we look and feel better.

SACRED WHEEL OF LIFE

On the night of 10th November 2020, I was watching the news on TV. The topic was 'Abuse...', and how there had been a big cover up. It upset me, and I felt very uneasy. I was about to turn the TV off, when a very bright, large figure of a really old monk clad in his robes appeared. It's hard to explain in writing what happened next. He appeared as sheer light, his eyes were set deep in his head, and the colour amber came around his shoulders and chest. Bubbles came around him, and it was as if I could see his veins he was so big. I was told "It all has to come out.

We don't help when we keep quiet. Cycles of Truth, he said, Symbology." He communicated with me telepathically and I 'heard' everything he said; he was very sad. He said he had heard that I had written a letter to the children of the world as if it had come from Santa.

A LETTER FROM SANTA TO CHILDREN

I hope you all received a letter from me in 2020. My elves had a big job getting all the letters out to you. But I hear many children did not get one, so this is for you.

I hope this year is a lot better for you all. We have all had a lot of time to think of what is most important in life; what is the best thing to do, and costs nothing. Some children have said that it would be "out walking, by the beach, countryside, parks, playing or cycling". We all love the great fun of being out with family and friends, and cycling, so always try to do it.

Even when everyone is back at work, we have so much to be thankful for. Our health is most important, more so than style or money, so always look after yourself and keep healthy.

When you are out walking, stop to hear the birds singing, look to see the squirrels jumping from tree to tree, looking after their young ones. Stop and look in the fields to see the Pat Bellied Pigs that are so big, also the colourful chickens, rabbits and horses.

There is much to see. Remember to strive to look up to yourself, no one else. Look how you all pulled through this year. You were great; you helped each other out and got together to do lots of beautiful and lovely things. It does not matter where you come from or what colour you are, we are all human and from time to time we all need help. Just help, no questions asked, then walk away. Be the best you can be to everyone.

Christmas 2020 was so different for my elves and myself, but we loved it, and had a great time. I can't wait to do it all over again this Christmas. My Irish elf gave his first Santa letter to a lovely boy with copper flame hair. He was in St. Austell, Cornwall with his family eating a pasty. The look on his face when he saw us was priceless, his eyes went to the top of his head and his mouth was still open with shock when we took off again.

So, keep looking out for us because you never know where we are going to stop. My sleigh has had a 'make over' by a lovely man named Zamme Nick. Zamme loves Christmas, and we love him. He has been writing to me for years, and this is my first letter to him.

On Christmas Eve 2020, after seeing all the children all over the world, we were still full of energy; this is because the reindeer and I had been recycled. To keep up with us, the elves had a 'spit and polish' and had a wash which is something they don't like. My elves come from all over the world; they are all different and are great. We have lots of fun tying to get all the toys out on time.

What if you don't get what you want? It does not matter, does it? Santa thinks something different would be better for you, so don't worry.

This last Christmas was so different, and we did things in a way we have never done before, but it felt good. So, it's good to have change, it opens us up to more things.
We feel happy to have seen all the children on our way back home.

THE NIGHT SKY : PLANETS, STARS AND COLOURS

As we took to the night sky on Christmas Eve, we were so full of energy, with bright colourful lights all about us. The night sky is truly wonderful.

At first, we played around a bit, flying through the sky, up and down, laughing all the way as we have done for many years, looking down at the earth as we go.

When you go to bed, remember to always look up at the night sky, and see the stars and the moon. If you see a shooting star, make a wish. See if you can spot any planets with your beady eye.

Like aircraft, we too have a way of getting around the night sky, and as we were all looking about, ooops! We came off track. My elves, reindeer, and I looked at each other with eyes and mouths open wide. We don't need to speak out loud because we communicate telepathically.

Suddenly, we could see all the planets dotted around in front of us, and we stopped in mid air to take it all in. Quick as a flash, the planets formed a circle and started to rotate, moving in and out as they went just as if they were dancing. There was one planet at the centre and another outside the circle, but with a string of light connecting them. The planets were moving and changing all the time, with lovely colours going between each one, touching one another, and changing shape. There were sheer lights of red, blue, pink, green, purple and yellow. It was so beautiful and peaceful with all the stars twinkling, as we all gazed in wonderment at what we were seeing. The colours were fantastic.

We took off again round a bend and then went to the right, when suddenly, the planets, all in alignment came over to our left side, as if by magic. They formed a line before changing to different colours (just like us). Some were coloured a beautiful silver, and some had different dots of colours on the lines around them.

What we saw was out of this world, so colourful. The earth is a magical place, so we must all look after it. We can all do a little bit.

I cannot put down on paper the wonderful sight of the night sky and the planets.

A VIEW FROM THE TOP

Oh "wow!" I'm on "top of the world!" Kathmandu looking out over beautiful colourful homes This place is so peaceful so mad and like no other place so wonderful. Tonight I'm going to camp on a high mountain. Tracking through the Himalayas with help from the local men and women. On our way up the mountain. If we needed anything from the villages the men would whistle it down the mountain. It was wonderful to be here. My friends and I all whistled, most men did. Now we don't hear it so much. Bring it back I say it's easy. Try it. Put your tongue down behind your bottom teeth, bring your mouth into an 'O' circle and blow your breath through your lips, ehh. I can still do it, (move your tongue about a bit) and wet your lips.

Now camping on top of the mountain tents are all up and the view is fantastic. After we had food and back into the tent it was dark I put all my clothes on and stood and walked around looking at the biggest moon I have ever seen. A full yellow moon but not like we see in the sky. It was like we could put our hands out and touch it, it was so close and the sky full of colour and the stars so so big. Oh Wow! Now all the shooting stars this was out of this world I sat most of the night looking at it all. I could see the sky moving to the right and things changing all the night.

GREAT DAY OUT & ABOUT

One day on seeing the children and their friends 'The twins' on games, on phones, on Facebook. I shouted to them all. "Right off with all that rubbish! We are all going out. We are going to see what is going on in the world outside, we will talk and see things."

"We don't want to go," they said.

"Get in!" I said and off we went. "Where would you like to go first?"

"America!" they shouted. Then with a thump! and a bump! and a few shakes 'off' we went flying high. Seeing dragon's on the way.

"Wow!" they said.

"Now we are on Brooklyn Bridge. Now we are flying over California."

A twin shouted, "I love this!"

"Right, now where will we fly to?"

"India," the other twin shouted. With that, a quick quick turn around "wow!" they all shouted and full of laughter.

"Oh look down! there are big elephants."

"Oh!" I said, "and there are lots of monkeys eating bananas.

"Look at the beautiful trees and long river," said Kaylem "and the sun is shining."

"Looks hot!" Anthony said.

"Where are we going now? I'm hungry said one of the twins." "We will eat soon."

Then Blue said, "look out the window the birds are flying with us."

"Right," I said, "we will fly to Nepal and Tibet." We did a quick sharp turn, bumping into each other.

"Great fun!" they said and "Oh look" they shouted. "The big mountains that's Mount Everest. Ohh! There is snow on top and it is cold there."

We saw beautiful coloured lines of flags and lots of YACKS!?. "Oh back home again. We've been out all day.

"What do you all want to eat? Pasty? chips, sausage and McDonald's twice?"

"Oh what a lovely day!" they said, getting out of the big box that went up and down and around the driveway all day!
"Phew!"

"Oh," where is Sky Lily?

Love life and live it now

THE OLD SHED

It's for one and all the family. Friends to share the good times. To talk the talk. Tell the tail. Have a beer, a smoke, soft drink, tea or coffee. Sow some veg. Sit down and chill or rest. Maybe sleep in now and again. To watch the world go by, to put the world to rights.

To do a bit of work now and again. Keep the tools in, pot things up and put them out. To sit outside and watch everything grow see the beautiful colours and eat the lovely veg. And on locking up and leaving, to walk the walk and always to look up to the night sky.

THE FIRST FLOWER

As I looked across the road to the garden opposite me. I couldn't believe what I was seeing. The beautiful colours that I could see; not only the flowers but the different colours around the flowers and coming off them. They were also going to and fro to each flower. I could see through the colour of each flower as if they were blowing in the wind, but there was no wind.

The day was lovely, sunny and very mild. Yet here I was looking at flowers that seemed to be dancing to and fro to each other. The grass was no different as it moved gently as if it was growing upwards. There was so much movement in the garden - it was alive and moving!

Then I went to stand by and look into a flower. I would say it was a see through flower the flower was alive with movement it was magical. It felt like walking into Anselly's toy shop. It felt wonderful. As I walked from flower to flower taking in all its wonder I didn't want to leave the garden.

All the flowers made "me" feel alive! I felt a great energy here and I didn't want to leave. It made me feel so happy!

We think we know it all but we don't!

THE GARDEN

Out digging the garden one day I accidentally cut through a worm with a spade. I was working too quick. I'm always careful and try not to hurt anything, So I picked it up on the spade and left it to the side of me and I carried on digging, putting new flower bulbs in the garden.

As I moved to get more bulbs. I stopped to look there was 6 more worms and they were all around the dead worm. I have never seen anything like it before. After a while I put them all back in the garden.

Then one night on putting milk out for the cat. The cats name is MR Boots and I always lookout the door at night and look at the sky and see what's lark-en about (animals) big and small.

To my amazement a worm was giving birth to a little one and within minutes the other worms from the flowerpots came out all around her I watched in the moonlight.

We KNOW nothing!

THE MOST BEAUTIFUL FAIRY SOUL ESSENCE

In the Menacuddle Woods by a lovely waterfall, there are so many big old trees. An old well, big old giant seat and a lovely little bridge to walk over or stand on looking down at the river. There is also a lovely wooden seat for the old soldiers who went to war but sadly never came home. There is also a lovely tree with ribbons tied on it, with lovely colours for loved one's lost.

It's a beautiful place here, gives you a lovely feeling and a good energy. I have been coming here for years. This was a beautiful sunny day, no wind. But then, there was a wind and the trees shimmered as I looked up. I saw a fairy in a cream dress. Its creamy, cut edges glittering. From the tree she put her hand out and golden string went across to the tree opposite by the river and she glided across. Then, she put her hand behind her and another line of light came down to the ground and started changing and coming into all different colours, all in the shape of a Triangle △ (full of different pastel colours). It was magic. Then she looked at me and beckoned me to come forward and stand in the triangle. As I did this, the colours started to change and move beneath my feet. See through colours, every colour I know, but not black. Ohhh!... then my feet started to move and I was dancing. I couldn't stop. The colours went all around my feet, up my legs, into my body, arms, hands, neck and head. I could see through my whole body. I felt as light as a feather. In amazement I looked at her and with her left hand full of colour, she put a White Rainbow all around the top of us. I could feel my eyes moving in and out with changing colour. So when you go walking in the woods STOP, LISTEN, LOOK, TAKE IT ALL IN and DO A DANCE.

Notes
Colours are within us. Very few people can see it.

BEAUTIFUL DAY

So boys and girls, when you dance, imagine all the colours you like coming into your feet. Then up your leg, going all around your stomach and backside, then up to your chest, then all down your arms and hands. Then touch your neck with both hands and feel it light up both your neck and shoulders. Then touch your head, face, ears, mouth, nose and eyes. Now you have lit yourself up with colour, your hair is shining and light.

Do this whenever you can and all your life, it will keep you healthy, happy and strong.

Remember the colours and circles change and move around, in and out of your body. Have a great time!

Use your Imagination

CIRCLES AROUND THE MOON

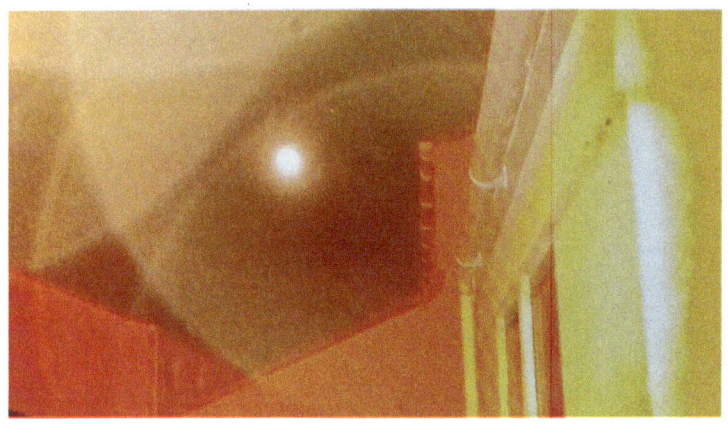

Looking at the Moon, over the years, the circles have changed with this full Moon different. Still circles but a different shape has come around it (like a bullet shape?) It's big and in the middle of the Moon. This is the first time I got a lovely photo of it.

Over the years the circles have always been round but more recently have changed to an egg or bullet like shape.

It will be good to see if it changes back again with the next full moon...

Always look to the night sky

THE ROLLING RIVER

While out walking in the woods on a beautiful day I walked by the river today the sound of the river rolling and rushing down over the massive boulders giving off lots of bubbles and seeing the blue/green colour of the river with the sun shining on it. It was just lovely and very, very peaceful. The bird song was just great. I even heard a woodpecker.

Then all of a sudden a grey heron flew down into the river and as I watched for a while he was looking for something to eat gazing into the water. Then after a while his long beak dashed down into the water then up he came with an eel (a long one) in his beak and off he flew.

There were lots of dragonfly and butterflies all around. Then as I walked on further, a blackbird flew down in front of me, as I walked he hopped along singing. It sounded lovely he flew off to my left as I walked on. Then he flew back again chirping away and heading to my left side again. He did this a few times. So I thought he wants me to follow him and I did. He led me through a lot of trees into a wood area and a covered up an old pathway and he stopped by another river. I had never seen this before as I thought (what a beautiful place). Then I saw bubbles coming from the water's edge. I thought (where is that coming from?) As I walked along the bank the water was bubbling all along the edge. Then "wow!" I saw a big salmon jump and then some more in the river just swimming along. It was just a beautiful day by the rolling river.

THE WHISTLING WIND

On a walk in the lovely Gover Valley (Cornwall). A lovely big viaduct with trains coming and going all the time children love it. At the start of the walk there was a gale of whistling wind. It came all around me and I saw a baby in pushchair with all the leaves on the big trees shimmering. We could hear the sound of the trees, a gentle whistling. The baby was cooing and pointing up to the trees. Then we saw squirrels jumping from tree to tree.

As we strolled on looking at the ducks and chickens in the field to my right a man and woman was there and said we could come into the field to see the chickens and ducks and the planting of new trees. There was lots of work going on, then a chicken laid an egg and the woman put it in the baby's hand the baby laughed and spoke (gobbledygook) to the chicken and egg. Then a long train went over the viaduct above us as we walked on.

A young deer came out from the trees looked at us and crossed the road to the woods he was so gentle. Then we were under the viaduct when another train went over above us it was a different sound and the baby looking up mouth open. Then we walked the wall of the river and we saw some lovely rabbits. Then the whistling wind had stopped we walked quickly back down the valley like "Grease Lightning".

PLANT (INDOOR)

My friend sent me a lovely plant for my birthday called 'Ficus Ginseng'. I never had one before. It was beautiful, green and very healthy looking. One day, I went to give it a little water and I couldn't believe what I saw. The plant was making a crystal pink and I could see it forming.

I took this photo as no one will believe this. What do you think of this? How could a plant do this?

WHAT COMES OFF A FLOWER

Plants, trees, brambles and nettles have a silver like substance coming off of them.

Colours and bubbles all in movement. Plant, flowers, trees - see through colours. So, so fine. All colours (but not black). Never black, even when dying.

RESPECT

The old granddad went to pick up his young grandson from school. He was having trouble with some bully boys at the gates.

The granddad heard the bullies taunting his grandson. The old man walked up to them, "What the f... is up with you lot eh! What's going on then?"

The big bully put his hand up to the old man. Ehh, he said, "granddad, respect to you."

"Respect! Respect?" said the old man. "I'll give you fu…. Respect!" and he chased after the young lad. The bully ran like the wind!

They never bullied him again…

WHAT TREES CAN DO

While out walking one very mild winter's day I was with a friend who was very sick. As we walked and walked around, I suddenly heard the rustling of tress to my left. A very different sound that made me stop and look.

We stood in front of 3 trees. One big and tall, one in the middle and two smaller ones to each side with brambles and nettles all around. The trees were still making a strange sound. We were facing them in the middle. When all of a sudden, the trees shook and moved and a "what" looked like a big white rope. "Smooth" came down from the top of the tallest tree right down to the ground. And the 3 trees "Aura! Colour" all white came forward to my friend's body organs, all around her and then back to the trees. She said she felt a shivering of her body. We stayed for a while then went off walking.

We saw a beautiful spider's web, full of colour. Within a few days, my friend said she felt so good. "Better than ever" I said. (One day, I will tell her what I saw)

Thank you to the trees.

The aura colour is what everyone has around them, all different.

Always go outside and walk about with your eyes open and mouth shut

LOVE

There are many ways to love. The "lovely" love of a gran or granddad. Much different from the love of a mam or a dad. Then the love of brothers and sisters, different still. Then there's the love of friends, different again. Then there is love for cats or dogs, so different. Then there is the love of one's house and the love of a toy, one that you keep for many years. The love of the land. The love of an old blanket.

I loved a black coat. It was old and not too good. But I felt lovely and warm in it. I felt good every time I wore it, till one day when back from school I went to get my coat and my mam said it was worn out and she had burnt it. "Ohhhh!", my coat?" I cried, and we couldn't get another one.

Love of plants, trees and horses. I love my hedgehogs and when they come back in spring, they come to my door. I look out for them every night. I saw them in March last year.

When I look at flowers growing, I can see the lovely colours all around them. Pastel colours like short ribbons and like coloured bubbles coming from the centre of them (the flower). Going around all the flowers, floating back and forth to each other. Then I went to look closer at other flowers and I heard a shriek. I knew the sound. A young boy passing had just pulled on some flowers and cut a big green leaf in half and I knew I heard it. I have seen a tree cry, weeping flowers, plants and trees. They feel what is done to them we all hurt but love makes it all better.

THE EARTH HAS A HEARTBEAT

We as humans, all have a heartbeat, so do all animals. We all have feelings. When someone hurts us, we feel pain. If we look after ourselves in the right way, we stay healthy. If we look after the veg and plants we grow, they look healthy and are lovely and tasty to look at and eat.

But, if we take drugs and don't look after ourselves, our body breaks down and we change, we get sick. Then it's hard to get well again. We need rest, good food and a lot of help. Well, so does our planet.

Our world has a heart beat just like us; but so much louder and stronger. I have heard it.

But now, the planet is off balance and it needs rest. Our rivers, lakes and brooks are in trouble. We are losing so much fish and so much land. Our mountains and cliffs are tumbling down all over the world. Our ice bergs are melting. There are not so many birds around and bees are getting scarce. Trees are getting cut down and forests are burning. We have to stop fishing so much. Stop culling everything and leave it for the wildlife to eat. Give everything a rest.

We never bought bird seed when we were young. Everything needed was growing all around us for them.

The planet can only take so much just like us. We need to know when to stop. Don't cut grass, let it grow - it's beautiful. Feed the birds. We need a good balance of everything for ourselves and our world. So plant, trees, shrubs and flowers. Let's make hedgerows for all the wild life. Don't throw anything in the rivers or sea. No, no plastic please!

We all need this world, so look after it. No abuse to ourselves or our planet.

Take all plastic flowers from graveyards and don't cut grass from March to September. Watch the wildlife come to feed and don't complain of long grass.

Be good to each other and it will work out right.

THE SUN

One day it was so hot. My mam said why don't you and your friends go to the beach. I will make you all some food to take and you can buy a drink on the way. I will also put some water in for you all.

So off we all went. Full of fun and very happy, talking all the way to the beach. We climbed the sand hills, played with a ball and had something to eat and drink. Then we went off again walking, looking at the different shells, crabs, throwing stones into the sea to see who could throw the farthest. As we walked on, ohh! We saw the most beautiful star fish, all swimming around when we got close to them. They were white, but all inside them, they all had different little colours in them. So clear, so lovely. Then we climbed over the rocks and then back to the sea. Then we heard, "Look! there are dolphins over there." Oh, there were 3 of them, 2 adults and a baby one. They came in and swam all around us. We could hear them singing. The sound was beautiful, nothing I have ever heard before. The dolphins stayed with us for a time, swimming all around us and our feet. We all couldn't believe what had happened today.

A truly magical day. I don't always do what my mam tells me. But I'm glad I did today. Wait till she hears about all of this.

Try to save the planet by leaving everything as it is.

Take nothing away from the beach or woods, leave it as it is. Only take lovely memories.

A FIELD OF SNOWMEN

One morning, we were woken to the shouts of our mam. (Ohh), we thought (school). Then mam shouted no school today there is 4 to 5 ft of snow out there. We fell over ourselves coming down the stairs (my brothers, sisters and me). We never had breakfast. We went outside. Ohh, it was so white, so fresh, so beautiful. "Right!" my brother said, "go get the Cottors, the Dead feathers and the Dockledays." "Nick names" for our friends. "Don't forget the Mulggens and the Fords."

Back we come all together, "get the Carlyons too."

The bigger boys and girls said, "let's get loads of old clothes, shoes, hats, caps, coal, sticks and anything you can find." Off we all went and brought back all we had found.

"We still need more!" my brother James said.

"Right!" said Cottor, "let's all go to the dump."

Ohh, we had so much fun, walking a mile in the snow to the dump. Playing snowballs, hitting each other all the way. It was so good, so much fun. We brought back old tyres, old rope and old bike bits. Ohh, we are going to build something (what I don't know). Off we all went into Hudson's field and all split up and got to work. We worked hard and all day nothing to eat or drink. The old dog was with us. Then when all the work and noise had stopped, we all ran to the bottom of the field to look and walk around and study each other's work. And wasn't it all great, just great?

A field of snowmen. All looking different, all funny and all great. Then we went to the top of the field and came down like a bat out of hell on the dilly's, the big ones had made.

Next it was all down to "Bumta's chip shop" to share chips. Then we heard voices, "where's my pipe? Who has my coat? We laughed all the way home.

PEACE

Peace what does it mean?

I was brought or grew up mostly with just two religions (Catholic or Protestant) and we were taught not to speak to the other religion never. So we didn't speak to each other. "Why" we never "knew". We just did what "we" were "told" by the powers that be. I don't remember my mam or dad telling me this, only at school. Yet we grew up with some of us living side by side, yet never speaking. How sad this was? But then, one day I got terrible pain with my friend Moll out playing. And I had to go to a hospital in Dublin. I was in a big ward, very frightened. I had never been away from home before. After I had a small operation, I woke up in another ward. As I looked around, I said hello to all. My eyes then looked to the side of me. To my left a woman asked me how I was and if I was ok.

"Yes, thank you," I said. Then I looked to the girl beside her in the next bed. She was also looking at me. It was the girl from the other religion in my street at home. Well I wasn't going to say hello to her but I did. So I smiled and said hello. She also smiled and said hello back. In the days ahead, we all helped each other out in the ward laughing and talking. No talk about religion and it felt good. We were all the same in that ward. All helping each other out talking, helping, laughing. I sensed that is what we should be doing. But as we left hospital we had to go back to not talking. But we always looked at each other and smiled if we could. "Who put all this stuff in our heads?"

I have no tag on my back now. I have no religion and much happier but I believe in God not man.

We are all the same but a bit different and that's great. I love it!

There is only one race – the human

HOLIDAYS

My uncle had a lovely rowing boat and in the holidays my sister would row us up the river bank, a long river. Maya was better on the oars than I was. I could never row straight, I would go in to the sides of the ban! But she was good at it and always pulled the boat straight up the river. We would stop by the side of the bank, pull the boat in and then go and look for mushrooms. There were loads growing in the fields and banks by the river's edge. There were also lots of wild flowers, we would pick and bring home to mam. When we picked enough, we got back into the boat and would row further on. Then we would stop again and go on to pick blackberries or whatever else we could find. As we walked further on, we could see the Salmon jumping out of the water. There were lots of fish in the river. Then Maya put her hand in the water and caught a big Salmon. Oh, we were so happy. Fresh fish are beautiful and look so white. When cooked, just boiled with a little salt I can taste it now! Sometimes people would ask my sister to take them up river for a trip. They would pay her and she would give the money to my uncle Jimmy and Bill Manifold his friend. The two of them would clean and paint the boat.

But one day we went further on and there was a beautiful white horse on the bank. We pulled in to talk to the horse and the man with him and he said we could have a ride on the horse bare back. This horse looked as if he could talk to us, he even looked around to see us get on his back – he was so gentle!

Oh, this was best day ever!

THE BEAUTIFUL HORSE, CART & YOUR FUTURE

My cousin's home on holiday so we would go out and about selling potatoes, fruit, veg., coal and sticks. It was great we would be out all day long. We learnt so much about growing, cutting and selling. Most of it all gone now sadly. Indy race loved the horses. But, you all have your whole lives ahead of you. I wonder what life has in store for you. Things always crop up life is not straight and we can't always make it right, but we can try.

(YOU ARE THE FUTURE.)

When you all get jobs and get a lot of money, please, please don't buy 2nd homes in the country or by the sea or anywhere around the world. So many people buy 2nd homes and are only in them a few weeks a year in the summer. But then in winter time the homes are left empty and there are not enough people around to keep banks, post offices, shops open and so they close leaving people here living with very little and sometimes no homes left for sons or daughters to live in. But lots and lots of houses and flats are left empty. It's causing problems all over the world!

If you need a holiday use B&B's, hotels or caravan parks. There are plenty to choose from and you would be helping people stay in jobs all year round not just summer. We must think about all these things. So, do the right thing. Always, you all will come out better in the end.

I'm thanking you all now for the future.

THE EARTH'S CRUST

Our Earth is huge. A big round circle. Its beautiful and you can imagine all the comings and going's all over the world. But now, it needs help from all of us. We want no more wars, no more fighting and bombing, no more Missiles. It is not doing the planet any good at all.

The powers that be should "know" this. But its falling on deaf ear's and we will pay the price, what are they thinking?

This is our planet and 'Right through' "the centre of it". It has "cracked". It is "breaking away from the crust" in the shape of a "Y" only sideways and it was moving apart as I was seeing it - quite a gap.

**We can change this, if we act now.
Not tomorrow, but now!**

Further Reading

We recommend the following positive books :

**Chicken Soup for the Soul
(by Jack Canfield)**

**Peace
(by Paul Keller)**

**Peace 2U
(by Paul Keller)**

Printed in Great Britain
by Amazon